Poems from the Straight Path
A Book of Islamic Verse

Poems from the Straight Path
A Book of Islamic Verse

JOEL HAYWARD

White Cloud Press
Ashland, Oregon

White Cloud Press books may be purchased for educational, business, or sales promotional use. For information, please write: Special Market Department
White Cloud Press
PO Box 3400
Ashland, OR 97520
Website: www.whitecloudpress.com

Cover and Interior Design by C Book Services

First edition: 2017

Printed in the United States of America
16 17 18 17 18 19 20   10 9 8 7 6 5 4 3 2 1

Library of Congress Cataloging-in-Publication Data
Names: Hayward, Joel S. A., author.
Title: Poems from the straight path : a book of Islamic verse / Joel Hayward.
Description: Ashland, OR : White Cloud Press, 2017. | Series:
        Islamic encounter series
Identifiers: LCCN 2016048664 | ISBN 9781940468532 (paperback)
Subjects: LCSH: Islamic poetry. | BISAC: RELIGION / Islam / General.
Classification: LCC PR6108.A98 P64 2017 | DDC 821/.92--dc23
LC record available at https://lccn.loc.gov/2016048664

Dedication

I dedicate this book to a good man,
my father John Hayward

"He was five foot four but I knew him as Goliath"

Contents

Introduction

I wrote this book for the Lord but I dedicate it to the memory of my father, John. My last conversation with him was a very cheerful phone call in June 2015 from the United Arab Emirates to New Zealand on the day before he died. I had actually talked with him twice that week, both times happily, but our final chat was wonderful. He made me laugh. "I don't understand something," he told me. "Everybody at the pub has stopped talking with each other. What are these little black devices everybody stares at and taps rather than talking to each other?" At first I wasn't sure what he meant. What little black things? Then it dawned on me. When I told him they're mobile phones, he just said, "Oh, right". Clearly technology had passed him by.

Dad was a bit troubled, but he was also a scrupulously honest, deep, reflective and positive man full of respect for people. He was tolerant and charitable and frequently asked me how I was enjoying Islam, the religion I had embraced years before. He told me often about the Muslims of Malaya whom he had met when fighting there with the Army in the 1950s: "Bloody nice people," he would say, adding that Islam had made a positive impression on him. Indeed, his very last words to me moved me to tears. After telling me he loved me, and me replying that I loved him too, he asked me what I was going to do that day. I told him I would go to the mosque for Friday prayers. My Christian father's reply was beautiful. "Give my love to Allah," he said, adding: "If he's your God then he's my God too."

My own religious and intellectual journey actually owes a lot to Dad's influence. He saw early on that I was a ceaseless reader and made sure that books were always included in my birthday and Christmas presents. No wonder I became an academic. He was equally curious about almost everything. He always asked about the people, wildlife and landscape where I was living. One of the very reasons I chose to move to the Middle East was because he had encouraged me to watch the film *Lawrence of Arabia* on television as a boy. It had clearly inspired him. "Endless sand," he would say. "Can you imagine that? Endless sand." I *could* imagine it. The desert ended up drawing me like a magnet and now I live in the beautiful United Arab Emirates surrounded by endless sand.

Despite his challenges he was a good father and when I was very small he was my first "prophet". Tender and paternal, he kissed my siblings and me goodnight even until we were late teenagers and he never stopped supporting all our creative activities. Dad always read my books and other scholarship enthusiastically and expressed pride in my efforts. In 2012 I unintentionally hurt him with a poem I had written about him, but he loved the book nonetheless and when I said I would remove that poem if the publisher did a second edition, he asked me to leave it in. "If that is how you see me," he said, "leave it in. That's probably how I really am."

Poetry is truthful; well, it should be. If we write it well it should convey as much truth as photographs. I always think the key, however, is never to reveal the photo too early, but rather to see the unfolding poem as the assembly of a jigsaw puzzle. With just a few lines, or pieces, in place, what will emerge is up to the reader's imagination. Hopefully in every poem an "Oh I understand" moment will occur. That is not to say that the reader should always, or even ever, get the same meaning as the poet intended. I like to think that when I'm baring my soul I don't have to parade it naked, but can hide it in the shadows at least a bit. It may even be better for the reader to dress the poem in whatever meaning he or she wants to give it, regardless of whether that meaning even remotely resembles the author's intention.

The word "intention" should not be understood to say that poetry is predominantly, or even substantially, the product of intellectual craftsmanship; the careful, calculated placing of words to express only reason. Poetry is neither domesticated nor feral. It is wild and free; born in the imagination, living outside the fences and boundaries of rationality and feeding on God-knows-what. The imagination is itself a wondrous gift from Allah which in the case of poets He untethered from the intellect and only loosely and occasionally joined to feelings.

Poetry should have a certain magic for the poet. Even what seems to be the giddiest and most frivolous of images can carry profundity, and the inner rewards can be immense. For this collection I wrote a poem, *The wind was my teacher*, and gave it these opening lines: "My soul is an empty crisps packet / caught in the sour mood of a shouting wind". I was trying to paint one bright burst of religious inventiveness in words, effectively saying that I imagined the Lord taking my soul on a mad, head-over-heels journey something like the Night Journey on which the Holy Prophet Muhammad ascended to Paradise. I saw the Lord lifting my soul as effortlessly as a hurricane would snatch away a paper bag. I saw my own soul, by comparison, as being utterly unworthy of His attention, so I painted it as an empty crisps packet. My wife considered this to be appealing and clever imagery but a strange choice. The very next day, however, I was astonished to see a bird flying purposefully above the Bawadi Mall in Al Ain with an orange crisps packet in its beak, presumably taking it to use in the construction of a nest. This was almost an ecstatic moment; as if the Lord was saying to me, "I like what you did with that poem."

I am not so arrogant to believe that the Lord of the Worlds does like my poetry, but I write most of it directly to Him; that is, imagining that He's my only reader. I write it as repayment of His clemency and as prayer. It is confessional. It is cathartic. I also write it as something less solemn; as a way of telling Him how I'm feeling about the world around me. Of course, He knows every feeling before I have it, and nothing in the world has escaped His view anyway. Yet the feeling of needing to tell Him can't be contained so I let the words bubble forth. In this book I have placed 99 poems, one for each of His glorious names.

I certainly became a Muslim at a difficult time for Islam, with tensions between Muslims and non-Muslims severely strained by 9/11, the subsequent "War on Terror," the so-called Arab Spring and its wars, floods of unwanted and untrusted refugees, the ubiquitous fashion of suicide bombings, burkas bans in Europe, Qur'an burnings, the rise of anti-Islamic groups, and a plethora of new books which wrongly condemn Islam as martial, backward and incompatible with modernity. I can't help but wonder what our Holy Prophet would think and feel if he were to see today's world and what even many of his own followers have become.

As a poet, my embrace of Islam could not have occurred at a more stimulating and colorful time. Everything *seems* intense; everything *feels* intense; most things *are* intense. I therefore thank the Lord that, in an era bursting with dramatic things to write about, he opened my eyes to the majesty and profundity of the Qur'anic revelation. I am a very fortunate poet. I pray insha'Allah that my poems on the state of the troubled and divided Ummah, on the wicked suicide bombers and terrorists who claim to serve the same God as me, and on the difficulties of staying on the straight path in a world of distractions and challenges, have captured at least some of the reality of today's troubled Islamic world.

Poets often pride themselves on the cleverness of their words, in a rather self-satisfying way without much regard to any greater purpose. I suspect that I've been like that myself at times. May the Lord forgive me for my ego; I wrestle with it like all humans. My goal with this book is hopefully more worthy: I want to honor my Creator; to paint in words the mystery, incomprehensibility and resplendency of radiant Allah subhanahu wa Ta'ala with a palette of dazzling verbal colours.

Joel "Yusuf" Hayward
Abu Dhabi
2016

Listening

Allah is the great silence
the unconquerable quietness

inside and beyond a universe that creaks
moans and shrieks

Emptiness obeyed a single word, "be"
and became an impenetrable fullness

Time began ticking
babies began crying
soldiers call
for their mothers
when death embraces
them

He owns the East and West
and you will see His face
everywhere you turn

He watches, listens
and is silent

Some say He is the
shout of nature
the volcano
the tornado
the earthquake
the tsunami
the blizzard

He is not
They have
their own voices
His gift

Listen to Him in your soul
Be still
be empty
become the void
drawn near to
death
and listen

and there you might hear Him

Answering His call

A tap tap at the
window of my soul
saved me from
a life lived in the
wrong city

A hummingbird tapped
with the persistence of a
Mormon missionary
until I opened to let him
bring me a curious thought
in his beak

A pearlescent
sunflower seed,
the thought grew
day after day
until my soul
was a field of yellow
flowers standing high
like meerkats

My soul sneezed
and sent that idea
sailing to my mind
which weighed it on
Solomonic scales
and found it
weighty enough
after two long years
of questioning and study
for my lips to utter:

I need to become a Muslim

Shahada

A cat licking
its new-born
and blind
kitten
is how
the Qur'an
loved
and bathed
my soul

A falcon
feeding its young
from its beak
is the way
the book
sated
my
hunger

A stream of words
passed through
my mind
like a
typewriter
ribbon

living water

I drank words
to overflowing

and let them

spill

to an imam
with the heart
of a kitten
and the looks
of a falcon

There is no god
but Allah

Muhammad is
the messenger
of Allah

The strangest journey

I found a door shaped like my mother
I pressed against it and fell
into a room full of sunlight
cushions and songs

I stayed a while before
curiosity seduced me
like a cat seeing any twitching thing

The door shaped like my father
wouldn't open when I pushed

I searched for the key and found it in a bottle
The room was messy and a light bulb flickered
but great leather books covered the walls. I read
until my mind hurt like a belly full of steak

I peered through a window shaped like me
into a gloomy, empty room. Wait, a small boy
with the face of a philosopher frowned
in the corner. I'll come back for you
I shouted

The little door shaped like my darling
opened like Aladdin's cave

Her perfume pulled me inside
with a rip current. I swam in warm music
and kisses vowing never to leave

There's another door
I'll take her hand. Maybe she'll lead
It has no shape just a welcoming call

You have touched me

I could boil an egg in my hand
and melt asphalt with footsteps
as I walk to You, O Lord

O I will run

I am aflame

I have seen Your kingdom
in a bright blue dream
in sagging clouds before rain
in the slippery birth of a foal
in the eyes of mercy

My heart is aflame

I heard You call
in breaking waves
in the wide ocean's silence
in the cry of gulls

in an echo in my heart

We touched the Kaaba

We touched the Kaaba at the same time

at that very moment planned
before the universe
began its exuberant
laughing spread

by the Great Mind which placed a whale
in the path of a drowning sailor

a pharaoh in a collapsing sea

an excited stone in the brow of a giant

a quiet word in the belly of a virgin

all planned before the first sunrise

before the sun

We touched the Kaaba

and the Kaaba joined
our souls in marriage

Death

I heard the sound of a bicycle bell
deep within me

I listened carefully and it rang again
and I caught the sound more clearly:
a church bell

But I am not a Christian and the last time
I sat in a church I heard that God had died
so I never went back

When that darned thing rang again
I knew it was a door bell
so I opened and the moon
asked to come in

Why had the priest upset you? she asked

Hear O Israel, the Lord Your God,
The Lord is One, I told her

I had learned it years before I ever shaved

The moon embraced my soul
and went to leave

One more thing, she said, like an afterthought
Would you like to come with me?

My soul left with her

Jinns dance in the desert

Sand wisps dance across the road
Jinns crossing to find their tents
in the desert's empty heart
relax in God's grace

Scorpions join them in joy
and they rule the world
bi'ithnillah that would send me
in an hour to the next life

O Lord of the Worlds
when I see the jinns dance
I think of scorpions
and angels

and Your glory

and the one You sent
to possess me

enslave me

who treats me
like a prophet

whom I love
more than
life

Arabic

A small book
with the fragrance
of freshly turned soil
the spark of the Big Bang
the sweat of humanity

calls and weeps

Forests and deliverance
spring up where
the
drops
fall

all in Arabic

A billion Muslims
with wet feet
drip prayers five times
each day
in mosques
and secret places

all in Arabic

The Lord smiles

The devils who pull
triggers and leave
streets slick
with blood
shout

in Arabic
Their souls

take offence
at the words
of their
lips

I seek the happiness
of heaven
and read and pray
in that
dancing
tongue

But deep inside
in that strange
slippery space
where my soul
and mind meet

and my heart
bleeds

for my conscience

I hear the sound
of running water

God does not speak
there in Arabic

The Hajj

We floated through the pilgrimage
as astronauts in ihram with the sorest legs
and our feet sacrificing blood

Surreal and psychedelic touches
of the divine crowded our minds
under the same saluting stars that had
formed a crown for our Holy Prophet

Serenity in a crush of humanity and filth?

Madness! Madness! Shoving, trampling
elbows as weapons and the eyes of zombies

And beggars as mercenaries
touching, pulling, pretending

thieves and pickpockets

Fagin in two seamless cloths

hearts as unchanged by the truth
as the ISIS devils in those ruined cities

taking what belongs to the true sufferers
the noncomplainers who will feast
at the Lord's banquet in Jannah
insha'Allah

They plod to Muzdalifah on elephantine feet
more cracked than the skin of Death Valley

Honest faces black round Asian thin
smiles and brotherhood
floating in spacesuits

tethered to the Lord

the Ummah as a reality — nearly

The shadowless Prophet

I crept like Bilbo beneath the mountain
to see the Holy Prophet's feet

I'd heard them say that the man of light
walked without any shadow dragging behind

I lugged mine around as a burden with
the weight of shackles and chains

I stalked him like a cut-throat and
drew near unseen

O he sat and chatted with a wife
who combed his beard and fussed

Her laugh was a bubbling brook
his voice the Grand Canyon

I crept closer to where I might see
how he joined the grateful Earth

His words rumbled as an earthquake
The walls of the mosque trembled

So did I

He stood and bade her farewell with a kiss
and I felt it caress my own soul

O his subtle twin stretched from his feet
My heart sank like Jonah's ship

The man of noor's shadow whispered to me
What did you really think? That he is divine?

O Prophet I called across the world
Forgive me! I believed a lie about you

A smile stretched across Arabia
and he reached out to take my hand

My brother, the key is not to worry
about the shadow of the body

Seek instead for a shadowless soul
Let it never drip darkness on the faces of friends

He crushed me in a wrestler's hug

Falling into the sun overcame me
I swooned like a bride at love's first kiss

I drifted glowing in the radiance
of the blessed soul that cast no shadow

Bi'ithnillah

Tomorrow will give birth to a Friday sky
whose first wail will flutter as a ribbon of blue

Its new-born cry will stir the sun and the day
will begin with a mighty stretch

My love will call me from part-time death
dissolving my dream like an aspirin

Bi'ithnillah she will roll back my Van Winkle sleep
with the blankets — Lazarus, come forth!

and we will give thanks in the mosque
beneath a yawning dome wrapped in blue

The past

Memories are gravestones
dead things barely warmer than
the shrouded sleepers beneath them

Elegantly chiselled marble slabs
lettered in gold like graduation certificates
they mattered when first placed as the heads
of concrete bodies

Neglected like British grandparents
they reach their own old age

Worn, dull and crooked they no longer
do what they once promised

My mind is a graveyard full of
memories

I make sure I've left before dusk
begins his malevolent fun:
creating clutching shapes
and shadows that lurk and claw

I never enter after dark — willingly

Sleep has other plans, sometimes unkind
I am the wide-eyed boy it too often
leads by the hand through arching gates
into that deathly amusement arcade

Sleepers rise from their beds and re-enact
scenes that daylight had forgotten

Last night I couldn't find any way out
and panicked like a cat held over water

O Allah I cried out in my soul
Take me from this place

Light strode into my mind and
the shadows of the past retreated
as the French at Waterloo

It is daylight. I will keep my distance
and leave the past to sleep

Supplication

O Lord hear the cry
of a fluttering soul

Fight my battle
be my champion

My fear is a high flying swallow

My love asks me,
Where is your faith?

Honey, my faith is a straight spine
and an upward gaze

I know and believe

but I am David the giant-slayer
in the wilderness of Ziph
and my heart sings
a somber lamentation

I am fakir, the weak
nothing

My foe squeezes me
in his unwashed left hand

My own strength is
not enough to open
this blind man's grip

While I am weak
You O Lord are al-Qawiy,
the Possessor of All Strength

He enjoys power over me
but You are al-Muqtadir,
the Creator of All Power

Release his unclean hands from me

O Lord hear the cry of my soul

Love

I painted ambitions

Strokes as wild
as Beethoven's baton

lots of yellow, nothing dark

I hung the future in an oak frame
on an ugly wall

It enjoyed my awe for a time
sighed as a lover

met my eyes

blushed

We grew apart

I fell for a saint in black
the Hadron Collider as her halo

I painted her in delicate watercolors
as meticulously as pruning a rose

The future emerged in gentle dabs

Allah said hang her up there instead

Goliath — with a smoker's cough

Does my father live in a starving chocolate box
that sits and winks on top of the filing cabinet?

It catches my eye from time to time and I open
to search for my father's spirit

I find shriveled things:
small and nasty photos of the living and dead

smiling soldiers posing, flexing
machine-gunned bodies leaking like
rotten dinghies

The smell of regret and cigarettes rises
as a soul yet it's merely an imposter

He was five foot four but I knew him
as Goliath — with a smoker's cough

That damned chocolate box was his coffin
He knew he'd live inside it after death

He knew we'd look and feel shame that
he never deserved

Yet he never destroyed it. Truth
mattered to my dad

Beyond the odor of death and ashes
wafts the smell of freshly ironed laundry

My father walks free in pressed linen, a giant
insha'Allah in a world without memories

Mr Jennings

As hungry as a cat left in all day
I devoured a library and
spat out facts like fish bones

He saw an emaciated boy
from an Ethiopian famine

He brought extra books from home

I ate like Andre the Giant and drank
like Richard Burton

He patted my head

My hand rose like a V2
whenever he posed a question

He never asked, "Anyone else?"

I rained defeat upon my classmates
while my general nodded

We hid together at lunchtime
and talked of Caesar and Nepal

Born before the queen he has
sunk into the earth like old car oil

I am left to remember the man
who now stands beside my dad

The Prophet

Sunlight spread itself as thin as butter
and slept upon a bed of barley that the wind
lifted like the fur on a lion's haunches

A boy in the field waded in the breath of God
which rose and fell like carousel horses

He breathed deep and called to his master
Will you let me ride, O Great One?

The one-who-hears whispered O Muhammad
I truly will but tarry in youth until we reach
the chapter I have written for a man

The boy in the field looked at the sunlight dripping
breathed deep again and dreamed of galloping

On Thursday

It happened
on a mercurial
but affable
Thursday

sometime in that
imprisoning oblivion
before Fajr poked
my arm and said
go pray

I climbed
Jacob's ladder
as high as I could
— reaching only
the height of
Sufi egos —
before the
dead weight
of vertigo
and the fear
of Allah
froze me to
the ladder

I whispered to
bemused angels
for salvation

One with great
basset hound eyes
took me

rung
by
rung

down

a cat saved
by a fireman

to my bed where
I lay panting
with blistered hands

My wife stirred
and asked what
the Holy Prophet
had looked like

I told her
I might try
to see him
in the evening

She nuzzled
asleep and said

Give him my salam

We lay in Jannah
until the adhan
threw a stone
through the
window

Healing

Knowing that I was torn, You
began pulling edges together
Stitching them
O God it hurt

Stitch by stitch You closed wounds
while I looked away with gritted teeth

but said, more more

They say pain is the well of wisdom
I have drunk a full bucket
and am quenched

but I want more ... please

Great Healer most merciful
see my older brother

take Your needle and thread ...

She sits behind me and the road rises

Tightly pressed
together in a vice

we are squeezed and become
one cool Brando

She leans with me on bends
like a slow dancer

She is the road ahead
and I am the road behind

The engine thunders as a preacher
Her heartbeat is my music
my surging pulse

We slide between cars like we're
kicking open a saloon door for a showdown

For her I am a gunfighter
a slayer of dragons
an assassin

Our buraq, our steel and lightning steed
gallops through a frightened night

My love floods the road with noor and
all shadows prostrate

I ride like I'm being chased
but the devils have given up

We are the west wind
the bleeding sky

We take off our helmets
— tired warriors after battle

bow in leather in the house of the Lord
and give thanks for all things

Call to prayer

The adhan is a wolf howling in a dry canyon
to a moon

touched and weeping

It is reveille on a polished bugle to wake
soldiers from dreams and fears

It is a trumpet to announce the arrival of the king

It is a child crying for her mama's arms

fireworks to celebrate the defeat of the wicked

a kiss on the forehead of the soul and
a tender caress where it hurts most

seduction through curtains

the combination of a safe

a cowboy lassoing a prancing stallion

a lifebuoy's splash near a sinking swimmer

I clutch and am saved

and howl to an emotional friend

Moses

They walked through a ripped curtain
the colour of a jilted moon

Niagara falling on their left and right

The splash of shallow puddles
and the singing of praises

The wailing of devils and
the advance of a million ants

led by a prophet with a stutter

a love of honey and the
bitter taste of death on his lips

The Ummah is a barren field

It danced in a golden dress
beneath a contented sky. Suitors
called and courted

Now it has the all the joy
of a neglected grandmother
and nothing will grow but
disappointment

Bitter from its loss of beauty
at night it weeps black
and salty seas of self-pity

Locusts have swarmed and devoured
all wisdom and knowledge. Crows
have become vultures

The desertion of farmers leaves
a scarecrow playing king
but he can never be a caliph

Abel's blood cries out from the lifeless ground
but only the Lord cares

No-one else is listening

The Ummah is a wasteland

I will build a mosque for her

The Sahara has swallowed me
and I am lost without a horizon

The sun is an assassin cool
without a conscience

Life is this sand sea, shifting
and burying

You are close — an oasis
I can smell life

You are here — my wife
I drink and surrender in the palm's shade

You have swallowed me and
I am lost within you

I will build a mosque for you and
we will call scorpions to prayer

Things on my mind

My career is a baseball glove
— funny, I never liked the game
It lies on a shelf in the garage
curled on its back legs-up
like a dead beetle

Ever see an insect on its back?
As foolish and exposed
as a woman who's
just proposed but he said no

I don't want to dust it off
to admire it, slip it on

or imagine that I jump to catch
one popped into the outfield

I just look and recall its
beauty when it came wrapped

and the fun I once had
with my dad's slow arm
in the yard

My life is a fishing pole

I wade in a glacial lake
— dead insects float

An unfamiliar reflection smiles at
what I have become — a dreamer

My world is an Arabic book and a vision

I cast with the hope of catching the future

Fajr prayer

Sleep disrobes
shyly with the
coyest eyes

Tonight she is early

She takes my hand
and we waltz

kisses my eyelids
my forehead

I am unglued

We are one

lost

I reach for her
before dawn

I feel the warmth
where she lay

She is gone

I wash and bend
to pray

to thank

She kisses my eyelids
breathes on
my neck

Has she sensed
that my mind is
with another?

She slips from
the room again

I feel her

close

gone

It's very strange

A caliph trembles at the sound of aircraft
like a dachshund beaten too much while
his pack snap and bite and cock their legs
to pee on a better world

Their state is a chewed thighbone
covered in flies yet they mint coins
in gold and silver and praise God as they
throw effeminate teenagers off rooftops

A Turkish fisherman with a large shoe
stuffs cash into a pregnant pocket
and crams frightened souls into the shoe
which sinks on the horizon off Greece
like the sun

Assassins have the crescent moon
in their left hands dirty pictures
on their phones and tight vests
leaking lava

She searched for tips on eyeliner
the day she erupted as a volcano
leaving her sheer blouse to mourn
at home on the ironing board

The world has become as mad
as Napoleon in stiletto heels
cross-legged on the back
of a tortoise singing "Hey Jude"

The wind was my teacher

My soul is an empty crisps packet
caught in the sour mood of a shouting wind

She snarled and I careened
— a drunken trapeze artist

That moody spirit let me fall upon a mountain top
at the feet of a brick of a black man shouting

he has seen the promised land!

My heart cracked as an egg that slipped from the bench:
his people still stumble in chains

My shouting mistress carried me aloft and I fell
in the slit of a rock upon another summit
where the finger of God scratched Hebrew into stone

The wizard's face burned as the Lord's shadow
passed before him like the orange tears of a volcano

I know, I heard him call up to the Almighty. *They'll*
melt their earrings and innocence and cast a calf

Beneath the roar of my mistress's temper I heard the
wizard plead like a lawyer, *forgive them Lord*

They don't yet know

That temper carried my dizzy soul to another peak and
I beheld a young man slap the Devil on his left cheek

Get thee hence, Satan, he said, rejecting a throne
offered by that beauty with the stinging face

I heard the wind hiss and I cringed awaiting another crash

I broke my fall like a child off a bed and marveled
at the sight — O God what a sight!

ten thousand prostrating candles hurling shadows from a cave
and ripping sleep off a man with the bugle command, Recite!

My soul my soul! I am overcome. I begged the wind to return me
to my home and she took pity and swept me in a final gust

Let me hold your hand on judgement day

Let tonight open as a suitcase
as Sheba's red promise in the Song of Songs

Let the shyness of your lashes open
the night and convince tomorrow to look away

Find the map of my life on my desk and trace with
your fingertips where you think I've buried treasure

Mark it with an X. One day we will sail there
and I'll dig up what Allah put aside for you at birth

Become my mother but let me take your age
like that painting by Wilde

Your beauty will fill fields with flowers forever
while I'll age in oils and won't complain

Become my daughter with joy and madness
if my crown of bent tin ever becomes too heavy

Be my lover tonight and slip with me
behind a living curtain into the holy of
holies

Our blood is the same warm and flowing book
The ninety-nine names are our constellation

When He peels away this world and we stand alone
let me take your hand and speak for us. I will cover you

A hot frog leaping

My dawn prayer was a hot frog leaping
from my head pressed upon a prayer mat

It sought its master and swam in a pool of hopes
while I became the mat the grass the earth the ant

My prayer was a string of words the colour of
a Mayan sacrifice

It rose to a kite made from newspaper with
a tail of old nylons dancing in Paris

It soared and I let out more and more line
until it disappeared beyond the lip of my
knowledge

and another frog jumped

In Your good time

Let the thick and heavy
breath of the angel of death
caress my neck

while I prostrate
before my sovereign
in His glorious
emptiness

Let my surrender
be complete

Prayer is a standing
swaying kneeling
drifting
death
anyway

an emptying

with shallow
breathing

resurrection

Let the angel come when
I press lowest upon
my green mat

unmown grass with the smell
of the Lord's contentment

I am lowest He is the Highest
We are farthest from each other
yet never closer

I will sink into the grass
like water

I will disappear
into the earth

I will become nothing

O Lord resurrect me on my prayer mat

I am the bonfire you light

I bent the red sky
the shepherd's delight
into a triangle to dangle
outside my door on a string

I hit it like a bell when I thought
I wanted a wind chime
with a Chinese sound

but you came

You entered my life on a dawn
when the clouds burned
and your eyes were hot coals

You came in the wind you
were the wind and you
startled my soul

and when it said wowwww
you lifted that word to
the heavens and He heard

I drained the sky into a tea cup
yet you smelled of coffee
and I should have known better

You haven't sinned against me
and you've held me aloft as an
Olympic torch in a Spanish parade

You have covered me in kisses
like a newborn 'tho I'm old with
eyes which protest at morning light
You have read me Qur'an and

dripped prayers and scattered
wisdom on my head while I've slept

You have laughed at my jokes as
though I'm funny when I know
I'm a gravel road at high speed

Your eyes still set me ablaze and I
roar as a bonfire made from the
branches of the happiest trees

And wisps of flame and sparks climb
into the jealous sky while I snatch at them
to stop them carrying away your name

The moon is hiding in her pocket

She holds the sun in her right hand

and the deepest ocean pours
from her left as a Niagara of
dark expectations

flowing to me with words
that soar and swoop pecking
and clawing

O how I need the moon and
pull her close in a feigned kiss
while my hand creeps like a lizard

to set it free like that guy released after
thirteen years waiting for the chair

O how that embrace has wrecked me
as a car that followed too close

I pulled her tight to steal
what she had herself snatched
when the stars weren't looking

Her breath was red wine and I drank
and the weight of her breast on my arm
crushed my resistance

and I loved her again O as a universe

and let her keep it tucked away

My heart

My heart has no zipper
I've searched for a way
to get inside and remove
those sticky sins

My mind lacks one too
and the doubts that corrode
all virtuous intentions
— rust's passion for an old fender
are impossible to grab

I prayed for a can-opener and
the one-who-listens tortured me
with a jagged thing

The Great Aloner ripped me open and
in a month called experience I tore out
five weeks' worth of inadequacy

And your eyes? He asked

I'll pluck them out if they ever
settle where they shouldn't

In the Prophet's footsteps

We rode to Ta'if on a flying carpet
— a Toyota with a missing hubcap

sweeping through fattened clouds
which clung to the hilltops like grazing bison

arriving on the otherworldly plateau that wore
the death shroud of an old hermit's mystery

which our Prophet reached in sandals as bloody
as the deck of a Nantucket whaling ship

Arabian Himalayas. He climbed like a yak
and the Lord strengthened his steps

Our lost taxi driver poked at his satnav
and called his mates

The Almighty's beloved followed the angel and
never lost his way. He strained with pain

Our driver's mirrored eyes intruded while we
held hands on the back seat and yawned

The Lord smiled down upon his aching friend
and eased the pain in cramping calves

A sagging mosque now hunches where the ignorant
had cast away the chance of a lifetime

O think if they had taken him in — Medina
would sit as a happy king on a mountain throne

I immortalised my love in a photo in that mosque
praying as a saint where our hero had struggled

I adore my captured shaikha and the memory
of when we followed in the footsteps of our Prophet

The Great Soul barely spoke

— "be"

A rare and lustrous pearl
grew in the womb of
an oyster

The untouched girl
from a million icons

Satan winced
"O God, not again!"

Allah's reflection in that pearl
lit and warmed the world

for a time

Then He sent another

without a star and
the libations of the wise

To the one who came
and banished all shadows
He gave a slender book

which praised that girl and the pearl
and shook the earth on its axis

As close as I've come

I saw the Holy Prophet
Well, I stood in a crowd behind him
… on my toes

His hair was wet coal
and it shone on Atlantic shoulders

I remembered a story of a woman touching
the fringe of another messenger's garment

What could I say if the Holy Prophet turned?
I pulled back my hand

He never turned.

His eyes smiled but only in
the heat of my hope of our eyes meeting

His voice flowed as a Spring stream
I drank as a camel in the Rub' al Khali

The urge overcame me and I reached
— and felt your hair on the pillow as I awoke

I cling like a child to the leg of a mama

O the Lord is the flinger of things
the bringer of stings

the terrifier
the hypnotizer
magnifier

a spurner
a burner
the great turner

I am burned
I have turned
and painfully learned!

I cling to the Lord of all ages
sender of sages
the payer of wages

I hold tight

Live and love right

I cling

I cling

I am not a beard

I have enough
don't want much
more

Or try to change
anything aside
from me

Wouldn't hurt a fly
Ok I'd do that
but not a soul

Disagree with me? — I'll shrug
study it again and
feel I've done enough

I see your suspicion
I'd feel the same
but give me a break

I am not a beard

A promise

In my hands I hold your heart
like a sparrow

Don't fly

ever!

Your prize
might have come
in a shoe box tied
with old string
but mine came in
a ring box
wrapped with
blue ribbon

Will our love stay
as Abraham's fire
while time changes
the ways our eyes
greet each other
when sleep
withdraws
its faded curtain?

Will it survive
unbruised
during our
unmapped trek
through life
and the fatigue
of seldom walking
downhill?

When I am foolish
forgive me and
let my shame
form a jury
to find me guilty

I will serve my time
with pictures of you
pinned on the wall

of my soul

My promise insha'Allah
is to guide us
compass used
religiously

to the Lord's place
where we can rest and
watch a stony stream flow

You don't fool me!

When you come
you'll reach to take what
I've clutched tight

You've done it a lot
— especially lately

You did it to that unsuspecting lady
when she stepped off the bus
on Philpotts Road

to that sleeping girl
with the mousy hair in
the children's ward

to her father three months later

to my own dad while he prayed
by the bed and slumped

to that old pope who shook
like a wet dog in a sou'wester

I read again last week how you visited
the homes of those who wouldn't
splash blood on their doors

Now that's something!

I know what you want and I'm onto you

When you come I'll be ready — I hope
and I'll hand it to you without protest

But I have a request, if I may, and I hope
you'll ask on my behalf:

Please don't visit her before you call on me

Children's ward

Rainbows and more yellow

Balloons on sticks
— not the ones which pop

Sweet doctors and soft voices
soothe

The Lord watches us hide our tears

Heartbroken

I found you

The backs of my hands are ripples of Saharan sand
and a dark spot on the right reminds me
that age is a stalking falcon

My right side is aging first
Above that eye is a ploughed furrow
On the roof is a piece of unpainted tin

But the light from a shrunken candle is still
as bright
and I never knew you before all that wax
had dripped on the table cloth

O the strength and delight you have given me!
You have changed a late afternoon into
an early morning and I can't wait for lunch

Eat with me! Then let us read from the same book
and let our love of the sages form the yellow brick road
that will take us together to the source of all
wisdom

Knowledge

I snatched the ripest fruit from what
the asp found easy to convince me was
the tree of the knowledge of all things

I devoured its flesh and danced around its core
offering libations for a while

My mind was already a hoarder's house but
the thing
I craved — the hikmah of the Prophet —
remained as a shadow's footprints

Admiration for anything inadequate soon becomes
as pointless as a steeple on a synagogue

as wearisome as the purple noise of neighbors'
lovemaking

Lord forgive the hunger of a thief
— not taking a second fruit was his first hint
of hikmah

Her words

I am adrift on an upturned hull
lamenting misfortune

Her rushing words swamped my hopes
before I could turn headlong into them

I hate the horizon — that line of horror
that lifeless circle

My head spins beneath a heavy sky
which pins me like a sweating wrestler

Flattened and breathless I wait
for the wave that will drown me

All is lost

It does not come. The wind dies
and her eyes soften

She is calming

British Muslim

He ranted like a sandy wind.
"They hate us. . . . We're weak. . . .
O for the Golden Age. . . ."

So what do you want?

His answer leapt; a greyhound after a mechanical
hare. "The caliphate."
In his mind he saw golden domes: the Palace of
Osman and the harem of Solomon.

And who would rule?

"The Caliph of Allah subhanahu wa Ta'ala.
We need him. A great man.
Someone to counter the West.
Someone to unite and lead the disunited Ummah!"

And you would follow such a man?

"To the ends of the earth"

And what would his nature be? Like Al-Baghdadi?

"God no. He'll be righteous, just, powerful
and wise."

A new Salahadin?

"Exactly! A new Salahadin"

So what if he's an Indian? Would you follow him?
He slew me with a bladeless sword.

"An Indian? God no. He could never be an Indian"

Lord tell me . . .

Is it in that ulcer that recurs in my mouth?
that scaly patch on my right thigh?
blood on the loo paper?

Is it in the swerve around angry brake lights?
the crushed metal womb?
Will I be removed as a stillborn?

Is it closer than tomorrow?
Will it end a dream?
Better still, a prayer?

Do I deserve a warning?
— O God don't let it catch me by surprise
let me say goodbye ... and sorry

This new 'jihad'

Wickedness dances like a Chinese dragon
held high on poles by the grinning

It curls its tail and snakes around the minds
of admirers who see beauty in its gaping jaws

Flaccid and incapable, this billowing beast
intoxicates and seduces the frustrated and resentful

It dances in Kirachi, hoodwinks in Bradford,
and slips into the dark places in distracted minds

— this infernal idea more bilious and mephitic
than a komodo's bite

It dances wildly in the confused thoughts of lost boys
who haven't noticed its cunning wink

They sway and rock — utterly taken
far more mistaken — until stilled by the slap
of death

I would be David — if I knew
you were watching

If I knew you would marvel, my beloved,
I would risk it all with courage
that I'd have to pretend I owned

If I thought your heart would enlarge
I would strut in front of a mocking giant
and sling a stone with steely resolve

— I'd die if you saw how much I shook

If it missed I'd avoid your eyes and
pick up another and pretend the first shot
was only my warm-up

If I hit the brute and he fell
I'd stop myself from jumping for joy so
that you would admire this warrior's calmness

If you'd rush to hold me in your arms
I would willingly take a beating from
his angry fists — O for the joy of your soft touch!

If I had the faintest hope it would win me
eternity in God's presence with you, my heart,
I would even let that giant snap me like a twig

How do I keep her forever?

Slip her inside my wallet
between business cards and
stuff her deep within my pocket?

O God I lost a wallet once

Paint her in bright oils on canvas
and hang her above the fireplace?

I'd just stare and never want to leave

Lock her in a hardened steel safe
then swallow the combination?

Shipwreck us on Robinson Crusoe's
ring-reefed forgotten rock?

O Lord I know she's Yours not mine
but I beg You to let me have her until death

— I swear I'll do anything to please You!

then let me stroll with her on golden shores
within the world of Your limitless mosque

Tumbling in supplication

I slipped inside my prayer
and hit the bottom with a thump

Alice down the rabbit hole

I tried to open doors with keys that wouldn't fit
O Allah! Which one have You chosen for me?

I swam in the sea of my tears. Dressed in regrets
and shame I swallowed and choked

I struggled out of my clothes
and kicked off my shoes. Save me, Lord!

Satan called to me as a paddling mouse.
"Où est ma chatte?" I hissed back

He drowned in a clockwise spiral and disappeared
down a most unhappy drain

I smiled in my prayer and felt myself rise
towards an enlarging light

I thank the One who plucked me from the dark
and returned me to my prayer mat near the bed

The one in Raqqa

A vampire prince lives within the shadows of
broken hopes
and lounges on a throne of bones

A shy boy in shorts forgotten by his teachers
now lusts for the blood of those who didn't listen to them

Known by few and seen by fewer this
Robespierre unleashed
what he knew he couldn't control:
une nouvelle grande terreur

"Rivers of blood, rivers of blood," he whispers
to courtiers
who shrivel in his presence and pretend
to take notes

Minions hear nothing from the palace.
It's enough that they know what he would say
if he were with them

They shoot and hack in the service of a shadow
who asks them to kill and die in God's name

Their brothers' blood cries out from the ground
and in a rush of justice the Lord will answer

"What hast thou done?" He had demanded of Cain
What will the All-seeing say to the prince in Raqqa?

Tremble, O vampire. The Lord will throw open the curtains
and pouring light upon light will bring your sudden end

A day fast approaching

You see God's wrath

I see His grace

You see Him as a judge
and executioner

I love His clemency

You hear Him in screams
pleas
gunfire

the
digging
of
graves

I find Him in the sound of the rain
upon a tin roof

You smell Him in fear and blood

I breathe deeply the aroma of lilacs

Your God carries an AK47
and speaks in a loud voice

Mine is unimaginable
existing beyond understanding
whispering in emptiness

Yet we will both see Him
What will you say?

Iniquity

He pours his sin into his mug and stirs
Gulps it down despite its heat on his lips

He needs it — the day isn't the same without it
Loves the taste and the way it makes his heart speed

Enjoys it with friends who also need what it does
— even the waft of its aroma draws them together

Some take it strong or black. They crave its effect
Others whiten or sweeten it to lessen the
taste which
still sits on the breath as a pleasure for hours

He tries to give it up and darned well can't
— tells himself that he'll cut down. It's the best approach!
Yet even that's a struggle. Its aroma gets him
And it's everywhere

Who would have thought that such a small thing as sin
could taste so good and give so much pleasure
to so many people?

Wisdom

I bound my foolish ways
like a wriggling actress
on train tracks
in a silent movie

sold them into slavery

buried them in
an unmarked grave

crucified them
on the Appian Way

yet they live like a cat
and haunt and
diminish me

and the knot of regret
will remain tied

tightly

until Allah unbinds me
on that day

insha'Allah

My mind

Is my mind a garden shed?

I sit inside in warmth and think
of all the work I should be doing

I know where the tools hang in the shed

limp on nails like crucified slaves

Beneath that old tarpaulin is
a great idea waiting to be written

In a water-stained cardboard box is another
— the future of my career? —
weighed down by gumboots

I'd have to check them with a stick for spiders
— the result of a big brother's cruelty

So it's cold out and you fill my heart
with things I'd forgotten

Out the window I find
a smudge of darkness in the clouds

Our eyes dance together and I know
I'll stay inside

So much needs doing but ...
tomorrow the weather might be better

So much on my mind

Will a powdery butterfly alight on my skin
when I sit in a swaying wheat field in the sun
in Jannah?

I know what it would whisper

Will I shiver after splashing my face
and drinking deep from a silver stream
in Jannah?

Will I be bold enough — even the thought is too much —
to ask You for a cool home near a wide sea
in Paradise?

Will You let me love her forever — please —
and hold her delicate hand while we walk
the streets of Your city

Can we sleep in late after talking
about You half the night?

Can we Dear Lord draw near
to see You face-to-face?

Even once?

Could my heart survive the meeting
with Your majesty?

Could I ever bear to withdraw from
Your radiance and glory?

O Lord will you even let me
enter with my beloved when
we approach and tremble on that day?

Will You smile at us — our only hope —
when we flatten ourselves
beneath Your throne?

O Lord will I even guide her well enough
and my own laughable soul to
stay upon the path to the gate?

Will You mind — I won't — if she leads
whenever foolishness robs me of my compass
on that most difficult of journeys?

Hiroshima in a suitcase

Euphoric on a dancefloor

An arm around forbidden flesh

The fruit ... oh so sweet

The acidic shame of weakness
— the need to prove that you're better
than you know you are

The Lord sees your heinousness — that kills you
and you plan your redemption

You insist that when you do it
you will escape your carnal weakness
and enter a world where voluptuous
doe-eyed virgins ... the very sweetest
will welcome you with the hottest kisses

He wants it too
A solemn high-five
A brother's hug

Horror in an airport
Hiroshima in a suitcase

So you have escaped ...
What do you think now?

Cast into outer darkness
with wailing and the gnashing of teeth
and a devil's arm around your shoulder

Modernity

Your damned phone
rings in the masjid

The living God is calling
but that ringtone isn't His
Your lover fills your mind
and you hear her voice
as you fumble to silence
the destroyer of prayers

The living God is calling
but a frivolous melody
has swept the mosque
as a drowning wave

Our supplications sink
while we struggle
and the devils smile

Seconds of intrusion
— a mad jester at a coronation
The damage is done

Jihad an-nafs

My shadow bleeds
where I stabbed it but
lives despite my hatred

It crawled across the ground
to grab me by the ankles
and reunite with its beloved

The light is far and setting
and that clawing specter
has become a wicked foe

How bravely I sought its end
and how sadly I felt it slip
away from my resolve

Its cruelty only savaged me
after I had cherished success's kiss
on my right cheek then my left

I sailed blue oceans on balsa-wood
sought refuge in prophets' books
baked in the desert on a camel's back
yet still it came — a tireless pursuit

I beseeched my creator and He answered
by shredding my name like
a whip on an innocent back

My tormentor shrank and left and I only
saw it in the shadows fleetingly
but couldn't mistake its fixation

I cried again to my beloved who
removed me from the city's glory and
set me to work in a village in a clearing

It joined me in my reflection in a pool
where I had admired my mirrored beauty
and I recoiled in horror — we looked the same

I will turn my eyes from the admiring
close my ears to those who fawn and praise
and smother my inner voice when it croons

O Lord, save me from my shadow
Chain it in some dark distant dungeon
and may I never set it free again

She helps a poet

You leave footprints in my words
but they are better for your trespass

You pad into my perfect sentences

a black panther on a moonless night

I hear the tearing of your claws
and see what you have made of my poem

How can something so violent and so painful
pull a white rabbit from an empty hat?

Sweet panther sent from Allah
who could have known that I needed
you this badly?

You turned off the television before you left

Crusted dishes in the sink and the
empty packet of a microwave meal on the bench

Washing left in the machine and
an overdue bill pinned on a cork board

Trainers and worn slippers near an unmade bed
and a hard drive in the bin
pulled apart and beaten with a hammer

You drank milk from the fridge and wiped
your chin
strapped that thing tight and checked the mirror
and pulled your coat around your neck to keep out the cold

You left the light on — did you notice?
They found it on when they kicked the door down
and swept through every room far too late

Another bombing

Even Satan jumps

We are torn
an instant diaspora
the beautiful red
soon to be scrubbed away
— spilled wine on a tablecloth

Shrieks! O God, shrieks!
Gulls insane above writhing nets
or the shredded and shaken luckless
who writhe in the agony
of some mad boy's mistake

Sirens somewhere

Angels get there before
those who crouch in white coats
making promises they can't keep

The lucky leave in pieces
arrive re-formed
the journey made in a sleepy blink
like a child awakening on the back seat
when the car stops at the end

How long until next time? A week?
O Lord, another boy will lose his head
and sweep us up
in his own bloody mistake

Life is a contract

I swim in ink
blood thick
straining on a failed breath

Drowning wildly
inhaling a blinding pigment
touching nothing in spasms

Coiled in terror's ropes
a mind in panic
an inescapable end

The surprise of the bottom
a great thrust
splitting the skin

The ecstasy of opportunity
a gift of a breath
the purge of death

I reach the shallows
in a swelling sympathy
and promise more than everything

You whisper your own request
in the stillness of deliverance
something small: remembrance

On the way to the mall

Fingers interlacing

A focus
on those things that kill

Dissimilar hands
in the merest touch
hold a summer secret
and more than a selfish hope

The road and the heart disagree
on the speed of a moment that opens
to fill the miles travelled
while joined by that easy reach
of ageing white
and the strangest yellow

The world fills a void
of darkened glass
but can't squeeze into
two crammed hearts
which want the moment
to become the next day
and that most glorious of hopes
called everything

Red seconds and a weird
swerving madness
break that tender stretch
of glued completeness
but a resolute
unblinking awakening
pulls unseen stars
through the screen and into
that easy thing that
sometimes seems so hard

Such power

I ride Ezekiel's chariot
— a wheel inside a wheel
in the wind above my city
in the rain that lashes my tower
which trembles and groans in panic

A whining, shrieking spirit grabs
terrified glass and stone
with vicious claws ripping clothes
from raw and tightening skin

All my thoughts sail higher
and spiral in a heinous whirl
of paper, plastic and the terror
of the old and the small

My God! Such power!
The ox knows its master
the donkey its manger
and I Your call to bow down

Like nothing else

When you clambered above that
mudbrick circling town
did your stomach churn?

Did a sense of imminence
— fear of a furtive approach —
pound in your temples?

Did you press yourself, hard,
against the rock in the dark
when the voice struck you silent?

Did all colours fill the void
or did the theft of night leave you
blind and fumbling in a hole

Was the wind — wait, I can't ask
or put myself in your shoes!
I've never even stared at the sun
for a second longer than I should

or faced down the Devil

You are not as we are! Clearly!
I would shrivel and sag
in the light that enveloped you

I would be crushed — driven mad —
by the weight you shouldered when
a gestating word fell upon you

Wisdom that would drown me
guided you to a stony path over hills
upon which you strode as a shepherd
— at best we follow slowly and hobbling

So I marvel with wonder tumbling
at that cavernous moment when
you stretched out and grabbed everything distant

Yazidi daughter

Wheezing on a disconsolate mattress
face in someone else's stains
flipped over, forced apart
tearing the veil of the holy of holies
— Why hast thou forsaken me?
the abomination of desolation

Before in jeans, flares, a purple top
eyes noble, cheekbones ruling
bracelets and two rings
a gap between front teeth a
family gift

Bruised now, cracked and split
majesty beaten
the gap wider and leaking
winter goose-bumps on bare legs
and sluggish thoughts of expiration

The intrusion a raw desecration
a wicked weight
the crush of a salivary bear
the pungency of killing for joy
and a week without washing there

Vacant and splayed where
your sister had begged and
boy soldiers has crashed with
their boots on, you float
— face down and drowning

The world

I hate the harpsichord
and the lute and the pretension
of players who sit in the dark
and call it the past. I hate the past
and the cravenness of those
whose small eyes squint at the future
when the light turns on. I hate the hate
of warriors who love what they
see in rear-view mirrors as they
shout Allahu Akbar while they drive. But
I love you Hayati and the pregnant possibilities
of a mosque framed by scaffolding and
a quiet sunrise laying gold on your hair

The unknown

I cocooned you in a shroud
tied tight, and lowered you

The earth protested

The grave took years
to dig but only minutes
to conceal and I knew

I will never visit here
to lament your passing
and no voice will call me

I had cursed and damned
you, my nemesis, and
longed for this end

O the embarrassment! The
shame! What I could have been
if you had never fallen for me!

You took me in my prime
I was golden, special, but
you exposed my feet of clay

You made a fool of me and I
won't forget. You divided the
years before from those after

I hid from you every time you
came to call. Pretended I wasn't
home. You knocked without respite

So now I dance above you. You
are nothing. A shadow. God
you even looked like me!

But I fixed you. Beat you. Killed
and discarded you. I saw you
later where you fell. Eyes closed

No-one knows. What could I say?
No gallows await. But I don't
want them to see how I was

I am reborn. Aware how close
I had come to your triumph and
I detest your ugly name:

P-R-I-D-E

Together

You flipped a coin into the future
It caught my eye
a dizzy flash in the corner
a lucky snatch

"Heads," you had called
bit your lip to see
whether it would disappoint
and leave you alone

Thirty years in flight
caught in a blink
your forgotten toss
a startling thing in my palm

You had called it right!

A reward now bestowed:
the soul you had strolled with
before the beginning

The journey

Down train tracks at night
tightrope walking on a rail
hands outstretched and cold
a boyish imbalance

Shingle underfoot
wet soles slap a slow beat on
oily sleepers

Good-for-nothing moon!
Have you escaped? Deserted?
Overslept?

Stuck behind a black blanket
unable to touch my eyes
like Christ's moist fingertips?

Lonely breaths spilling and glacial
a bottomless swallow tugging a knot

My eyes are winter puddles

I walk towards the Big Bang

Waves slide up comfortably unseen
rattle stones in retreat
too close from comfort

Darkness reigns where Moses
said it did

Time offers no greeting
looks away
— disappointed or jaded?
and slips past me

as close as a razor
whispering with voices
I heard as a boy

Memories spin
— a zoetrope cylinder

She flickers there, my sovereign
the hoped-for among the hated
forgotten and neglected

In the void Dad coughs
— I would know his cough
anywhere

the gift of those slim villains

Their angrier brother
argued in every room but one
while we grew

Dad doesn't answer
when I stagger and call
but my cup runneth over
— I'll soon feel his hand

A slender warmth eases
beneath my collar
and the smell of bread
lifts a ballooning hope
that my trek will end

in a Homeric dawn
of rose-red excitement

with the Almighty smiling
saying, Rest now!

The way it is

I laze with legs a little hot beneath a quilt and buoyed
by three pillows
Someone taps tight a new carpet next door and I'm
annoyed

while the world beyond the plum curtain shakes,
burns and stinks of death
and devils shout He is Greater as they strain on
crowbars to force open

the doorway to damnation

A boy like a girl thrown
— frenzy and shrieks — from a tyrant roof
cracks and empties as they bray in a circle
and drop the rocks that are not required

Yazidi waif in a rag who saw her father beg
split asunder and discarded by a demon
who gargles and washes between his toes in hope
of an union

An imam falls on a street in a nation of bricks
sinful running heard from windows
brand trainers bloodied knuckles
the swell of achievement

I rise and ponder

— tap tap tap you bastards

then I pray

Jihadi

Hacking and slicing with your heart racing
while his stutters and stalls

You enjoy the sight of bulging eyes
seeing nothing

You hold your trophy aloft
proud of having crossed the line

A jackal called you from your comfort
and you flew to him

Parents crave the agony
of a reunion that cannot be

and loathe that grasping thing that grew
in you which you called

certainty

You know what you want
and you know how to get it

the world re-created
with enemies trembling

Does the taste when you lick parched lips
match the memory of kicking a ball to a mate?

Does the trembling blood-red mouth
of the captured equal the youthful hope of love?

Can't you see that only the weak tremble
and the strong are coming?

Smirk and boast tonight about your gains
Enjoy the spoils and grunt in pleasure

In an imminent dawn the hands of justice
will choke and squeeze

and a soft chalky breeze will take away
the harm you brought and your wasted soul

The accursed one

Impossible beauty
and a soft seat in the balcony

leaning over

feverish

a grave mistake
a pointless plea

a tumble and a thud

The world's voice
whispers

A crooked kiss
seduces

Piper with a snaking procession

First come
first served

Hope

From a bent nail in a grey plaster wall hangs
a moon which barely lights the frozen fields

Above another world the warmth of a midday sun
lifts wild blossoms beside a boiling brook

I step across the gulf each day
feel my skin tighten at the cold hand's touch

Needed in both I cannot stay where I weigh less
and struggle most

I cannot rest forever in the day although
sleep holds me tighter beneath that crooked moon

I cannot yet

but insha'Allah

the Lord of the Worlds will reward
that dangling disc with his greatest gift

and end my daily stretch across the expanse

More care

It slipped and shattered

a clumsy hand

a long silence before
a crystal burst
of wounding edges

Reaching fingers

bled and straightened
then picked again

Reflected eyes in
the depth of polished marble
search to gather
what will never be whole
except as a memory
of the first touch

It meant the world
when it held the future
and tasted sweet

Time reverses in a forlorn desire
and the hand catches by the stem
the shimmering meaning of everything

A steady stretch and a tender soul
place it again where it
can never fall

and the Lord says be far more careful

next time

Terrorism everywhere

A cold drop touched my head
and then another
my cheek

A run to escape
the inevitable
would have no point

Everything darkening
a low sky seeping

cold on my lip and eyelashes
and I hunch
seeing spots spreading

Winter without respite

A day of bleached sun

here
there

everything dying
strangers coughing

Who danced for rain
and gave ear to
the one who fell?

the one who kept eyes
from the book
while the screen hid truth

I see death in crowds
feel the wet ground slipping
taste a drop on my tongue

our world for a season
puddles icing
and Spring impossible

My father's journey

What colour is the emptiness

into which you slipped
when you fell in a slump
near the bed

and knew it had come
felt yourself empty

while rings of darkness
squeezed those eyes
which I miss?

Did it depart
before you could call
any name?

I see your photo
among ignored war books
and I know what your smile means

You spoke His name
while He and I listened
on the line

You told me to
give Him your love
although you're now there

and closer

insha'Allah

Your voice is lost someplace
in my sadness
but I'll ask a favour

give Him my love

Eve

Sweet mother of humanity
life is your softly spoken name
and it floats warmly on your breath

A sister and lover flawlessly shaped
from the whitest plucked rib
of the wide-eyed dreamer

The melting touch of fingertips
the concurrent exhaling of souls
testify to the magic of Allah's work

Alhamdulillah

alone and together
in a sunlit realm of boundless hope
and the nearness of whispering kisses

A silent world to explore
holds less allure than the sacred space
of dreamless sleep within wrapped arms

I rejoice at what He made from my rib
my greatest warmth in winter

You are the North in my compass

In a blue room

The sense of not being alone
on a prayer mat
red mainly and pointing to the bed
and to someone close and far beyond

crooked in a room full of creams
clothes on hangers
and desire
heartens a discouraged soul

together
no-one leading

whispered du'as
and the awareness of intimate touch
at the end

I know you'll look sideways
finding my eyes
when you return to this world
of inadequate meaning

Do you feel me shake?
notice the red in my gaze?
feel my mediocrity
and impiety?

Your smile
slight
at the corners
fills the truest moment

and we hope
on folded knees
for a future
given by the true imam

A mystery glides in black

You are a mystery

I have fathomed
and know

You glide in black
the walking darkness
a moonless night

The stars I see
are my universe
and they look with love

Their warmth touches
and a stretched hand
offers something

immortal

You

golden soul
opaque in velvet

the invisible obvious

pious perfection

glide in black

The future

The future
sat reading outside Costas
in the concrete shade
of a surprised November

A timid wind
now gone
lifted an addictive aroma
and stronger possibilities

A third face faded
as they talked of a shaykh
but returned to suggest
what she could not have foreseen

The future in a charcoal scarf
safety-pinned curiously
beneath a delicate face
and eyes gilt with Moroccan tea

or the amber of ancient Iraqi beads
squeezed and counted

sat and wove
a binding incantation
with words which crawled as a spider
balancing on a few first threads

while the Highest
blew upon the ready tinder
so gently that the first flickers
went unnoticed for a time

A perfect present
a gift
replaced the past's
soreness and stolen years

The future smiles
and we give thanks
for what Allah bounteously
chose for those whom He has joined

Your love

You slipped into the dark
and my heart enlarged
while the blinking dampness of joy
blurred a vision
of the slender angel who whispered

I am yours

in a moment of surprised elation

You my love
delicately entered a private place
wondrously separate and untouchable
and slipped your fingers
onto mine with a shared dream
as you had on the sunlit night when
you asked with lowered eyes and I accepted
with a stammer

Your offering — a veiled retreat from the eyes
of those who don't care
further into my soul's tightening embrace —
lifts me upon a carpet
where completed I thank the One
for someone as close to flawlessness
as He will let any of His faithful
sinlessly desire

Failing on a hot day

Disappointment is a toothache
the droop of an eyelid

Age and failure
cause a dry mouth to swallow

I try to hide
what I cannot and hate

You notice those things
I swore had perished

when I humbly claimed I was
another

You winced
as I dropped you at a bus stop

amongst burned strangers
without discussion

I found you in the mirror
as shame brought a dull ache

the throb of sin in my jaw
is the price of feigned wisdom

and the inadequacy
of my devotion

Happiness

I adored your hair
with my brush
and died
and wondered

how many
strands
of you
I would bring home

caught and treasured

I tamed the wildness
with my fingers
and tucked silver threads
beneath

Some I pulled
while you slept
against me
with soft breaths

They fell
forgotten in what
streamed through
gold curtains pulled tight

and I slipped in seconds
while your glory spills
as a cushion
on my shoulder

where you fit

caught and treasured

Where?

In my wardrobe
I fumbled in coat pockets
and upside-down jeans
which hung in shame

I looked with my head
on a tilt for the shape
in the blanket of dust
beneath the bed

I felt under the car seat
with an arm stretched to the elbow
hoping to feel what
I hoped was there

I searched fragments of the past
that clung
like those yellow things
unwanted

Did I ever have what I thought
I held tightly in my left hand
while I walked in school shorts

alone

and broke the ice in puddles?

I asked Allah
in a close whisper
if I can ever have
what I have never had

and He said
open your right hand

With a ribbon

That thing from the Lord

a reward

in a tiny box
tied loosely with a ribbon
which I undid
quickly

That thing inside
caught the light
threw it at me
and drew my hand
to it
with a slow question

I called your name
hoping for a full moon

The sun came
from inside
and I gasped
and blinked

for a second

I called again
asked for a sign

A wind rushed
from inside
and carried Summer
to my skin

I said Shahada again
in my mind
fearing death

alone

Peace came
overflowing
and full of the silver dew
of a morning after sleep

That thing from my Lord
belonged
outside my clumsy hands
which gently sealed
the lid and
tied a silken bow

I looked at the
delicate wrapping
paused
prayed
touched my lips
and undid it again

quickly

Ya Allah

My soul
feels
the pull
of gravity

My back
strains
to straighten

and doesn't

Why can't it?

Ya Allah

I am older
than
yesterday's promise

I am older
than my forgotten dreams

I ache
in prayer

My failure presses

Lift me O Allah

The bond

We sit in cafes
sipping
slipping deeper
concealed in corners

chair backs
as walls

averting all eyes
ours locked
hungry

The universe
in two chairs
touching

These spaces
our places
yet ... anyone else's
later

The future
in two chairs
pulled close
knees joined
sipping
slipping
true love

with coffee

In black

In black
and small
a doll with
eyes that seized
and held

me

in thrall
and wonder

In black
beside me
so close
this soul
and yet
my hand
curled

alone

In black
the dream
of years
in tiny shoes
with a power
unknown
except to Allah
and me

In black

Somewhere else

in the mosque

away
engulfing
my smiling prayer
with a clutching
presence

A matter of time

Woolen tufts
of undemanding hair
on your neck

Raised veins
across the twist
of your wrist

The curiosity of
your lips smiling
when you swallow

and your eyes
drowning close
to my nervous soul

touch it
warm it
lift it
love it

and the slip
of fingers beneath
your blue humility

The hushed sigh
that's too loud
on a bus

A whispered
truth from
a locked room

thanks you
needs you

calls you
and asks you

not to leave

Sunlight of joy

On a prayer mat
in a storeroom
we met
in love
and I groaned
with a yearning
and you reached
my soul

In a mind full of wonder
in that room
in darkness
I found you
complete

beautifully small

alive

Sunlight of joy
in a windowless space
and a world
without time
for a moment
gave us
a flicker
of our future

A union

Alone with fingertips
and lips
the world thrown away

Allah above and inside
our longing
as milk

A touch full of age

Ten thousand years
found in heartbeats

The world unwanted
for a few minutes

alone

A sigh

I read of the shadow
of the Valley of Death

comforted by Thy staff
wishing I had written it

the truth of truth

I scan the surface of the darkness
as a Muslim
frightened of the deep

In the void
I sat wishing I could write

with God's spirit

As a Muslim
I heard the crackling of a bush, burning
and marvel that
You are who You are!

I remove my sandals

As a Muslim I know
David picked up five stones
when one was enough

Allow me the gift ya Allah
that described the fall of a bronze sword

across the croaking throat of a giant

and please let truth flow as beauty

from this small Muslim

Call me Daniel

The Angel of Death
grins for a second in eyes
golden, pacing and snarling
while I crouch to run
and cry upon the Lord
inside a heart that cannot
push words forth for fear

I am Daniel

I ache with a failed gasp
while beasts
breathe hell's heat
on my neck as I await
the tearing darkness of
that lonely moment
of a crushing journey

I am he

Dead in the minds of
those who cast me down
to these great jaws and
walked away without
bothering to watch
the end of their evil
which they had enjoyed

Who am I?

Dead in my pity
as decades of mistakes
fill seconds of regret
and shame at failure
while I steady myself

for a meeting
with the All-seeing

Who has come?

They stretch and twitch
and lower their bellies
upon the dust and rest
with tawny disinterest and
closing eyes and yawns
and the pleasure of
the sun's warmth

You are here

I fall upon my knees
call Your name
and stretch my hands
upon the earth that
asks to meet my head
and heart and
I thank You

We are here

I look up at new life
and see tomorrow as
a wider world and
a place to walk with
a great friend who
will stay as close as
the easy breath in my lungs

Repentance

The mirror has nothing
to offer

no salvation

yet I only need to
see my eyes
when I wash
and my soul
groans
O Lord I'm sorry

My darling is
gentler than
a woolen jersey

yet just a hidden
glance at her makes
my impiety say
O my shame!
Slay me!

The book has the
quietest voice
like a sweet girl

yet I read of
the wages of sin
and my conscience
begs Stop shouting!

I am convicted
I am repentant
I am listening

You did your worst

You threw sludge in a bucket
Aiming specially at my name
You covered me from head to foot
Then jeered go hide your shame!

Ain't no mud gonna stick to me, my friend
When I bow down where I ought
Your filth ain't worth a thought
Ain't no mud gonna stick right to the end

You hated that I feared the Lord
It sent loathing down your spine
Faith is a crutch for the weak you thought
Your spine far weaker than mine

Ain't no mud gonna stick to me, my friend
When I step forward on that day
He'll know what I have prayed
Ain't no mud gonna stick right to the end

You lied and told them white was black
Turned goodness into something bad
Your rotten soul hell-bent on harm
Your hateful thoughts both sad and mad

Ain't no smear gonna tarnish me, my friend
When Allah calls me to his side
He'll already know what's clean inside
Ain't no smear gonna last until the end

Glossary

Adhan: The Islamic call to prayer. It is made five times a day, ordinarily from the minarets of mosques, to remind all Muslims that it is time to pray.

Alhamdulillah: An Arabic phrase of thanks and devotion: "Praise be to Allah"

Allah subhanahu wa Ta'ala: Allah [God], may He be praised and exalted

Allahu Akbar: An Islamic phrase: "Allah is Greater!"

Bi'ithnillah: An Islamic phrase: "With the permission of Allah"

Buraq: This is the horse-like creature that carried the Prophet Muhammad from Mecca to Jerusalem and back during the Isra and Mi'raj or "Night Journey," according to Islamic literature.

Caliph: A caliph is the supreme religious and political leader of an Islamic political entity known as a caliphate, which has sometimes been synonymous with the Ummah (Islamic "community").

Du'a: A spontaneous personal prayer

Ezekiel: One of God's Hebrew prophets, named in the Qur'an as Dhul-Kifl

Hayati: An Arabic expression of love which means "my life"

Hikmah: Arabic for wisdom

Ihram: When male pilgrims on the Hajj enter into a state of holiness — known as ihram — they visibly represent this by wearing two white seamless cloths, with one wrapped around the waist reaching below the knee and the other draped over the left shoulder and tied at the right side

Imam: Arabic for leader; ordinarily given to the man who leads prayer in a mosque

Insha'Allah: An Islamic phrase: "Allah willing" or "if Allah wills"

Jannah: The Garden of Paradise, the abode of Allah's beloved after death

Jihad: Arabic for struggle, ordinarily the inner struggle against ego and sin but sometimes a defensive armed struggle waged by a legitimate Islamic leader and his forces

Jihad an-nafs: A person's inner struggle against the ego

Jihadi: A silly phrase used in the West to denote a Muslim who conducts ideologically motivated guerrilla warfare or terrorism

Muslima: Arabic for a female Muslim

Muzdalifah: One of the "stations" of the Hajj pilgrimage

Nafs: A person's inner identity; the "self" or ego

Noor: Light

Rub' al Khali: The "Empty Quarter" is the largest contiguous sand desert on earth, located in the southern third of the Arabian Peninsula.

Salahadin: An-Nasir Salah ad-Din Yusuf ibn Ayyub, known as Salahadin or more simply as Saladin (1137–1193 c.e.), was the first sultan of Egypt and Syria and the founder of the Ayyubid dynasty. Even his enemies came to respect him as a man of wisdom, genius, morality and chivalry.

Shahada: The Shahada ("testimony") is an Islamic declaration of belief in the oneness of Allah and the acceptance of Muhammad as his prophet. In its shortest form, the shahada reads: "There is no god but Allah. Muhammad is the messenger of Allah".

Ummah: The Islamic community

Yazidi: The Yazidis are an ethnically Kurdish people with a distinct and independent religious community who live primarily in the Nineveh Province of Iraq. They have been badly persecuted in recent years by a vile and violent group which calls itself the Islamic State.

Ya Allah: Arabic for O Allah

Zoetrope: A zoetrope is a cylindrical pre-film animation device that produces the illusion of movement by displaying through slits a sequence of rotating drawings or photographs.

About the Author

 Professor Joel ("Yusuf") Hayward is a New Zealand-born British scholar, writer and poet who has held various posts, including Chair of the Department of Humanities and Social Sciences at Khalifa University (UAE) and Dean of the Royal Air Force College (UK). He was elected as a Fellow of both the Royal Society of Arts and the Royal Historical Society. He has earned *ijazas* in *'aqīdah* (theology) and *sirah* (the Prophet's biography). He is the author or editor of many books of non-fiction. Joel is also active in the literary arts. His first poetry collection, *Lifeblood*, appeared in 2003 to excellent reviews, and his second, *Splitting the Moon: A Collection of Islamic Poetry*, appeared in 2012 to equally strong praise. His poems have appeared in many literary journals and magazines. *Poems from the Straight Path*, his third major collection, includes poems about his conversion to Islam, his religious journey, experiences and observations as a Western Muslim, and thoughts on the state of the Ummah. It also includes more intimate poems on love, worship, and the struggle for the overthrow of the nafs. He writes his poetry to capture events each day in the way that some people keep a diary. They are therefore deeply personal, yet reflect the ever-changing world around him.